RIDING THE WAVE

A Handbook for Parenting the
Child with A.D.D.

by

Dr. Teeya Scholten
Registered Psychologist

3rd Edition
July 2010

Canadian Cataloging in Publication Data

Scholten, Teeya
    Riding the wave: a handbook for parenting the child with A.D.D.

3rd edition
(The good news about A.D.D.)
Includes bibliographical references.
ISBN: 978 - 9731247-5-0

    1. Attention-deficit disordered children—Behavior modification I. Scholten Psychological Services. II. Title. III. Series: Scholten, Teeya Good news about A.D.D.

RJ506.H9S36 1998   649'.153   C98-900864-9

Scholten Psychological Services,
Box 923, 105 - 150 Crowfoot Cres. NW,
Calgary, AB. T3G 3T2
e-mail: teeya@shaw.ca
www.GoodNewsAboutADD.com

Year of this printing: 2010   (2)
Published privately in Canada

RIDING THE WAVE

A Handbook for Parenting the Child with A.D.D.

Dr. Teeya Scholten, R. Psych.

Author of the

"Good News About A.D.D." Series

Other books in this series are:

- "Attention Deluxe Dimension": A Wholistic Approach to A.D.D.

- The A.D.D. Guidebook: A Self-Directed Guide to Understanding A.D.D. in Adults and Children

- Welcome to the Channel Surfers Club!
  (Primary Version)

- Turning the Tides: Teaching the Student with A.D.D.

- Overcoming Depression: Wholistic Strategies that Work

Co-author of:

Ready-Set-Go: A Three Step Problem-Solving Process for Improved Learning Performance

CHILDREN

They come through you but not from you

And though they are with you

Yet they belong not to you.

You may give them your love

But not your thoughts.

Their souls dwell in the house of tomorrow

You may strive to be like them

But seek not to make them like you…

You are the bows from which

Your children as living arrows are sent forth…

Let your bending in the Archer's hand

Be for gladness.

Kahil Gibran
The Prophet

ACKNOWLEDGEMENTS

I wish to thank the original researchers for identifying the importance of focusing on the development of self-control in ADDers. Barb Blakemore, Simone Shindler and Dr. Richard Conte were my colleagues and I learned a great deal when I was working with them.

To all of my friends and colleagues who have given feedback on this book. To Elissa Collins Oman, an editor par excellence and Dr. Heather MacKenzie, S.L.P. for being a continual supporter and inspiration. Heather has contributed significantly to this third edition in her editing suggestions and writing the Foreword to explain the importance of finding ways to teach our children self-regulation. To John Breeze of the UPS Store for his artistic taste, professionalism and perseverance in producing beautiful products. Thank you all so very much.

To all parent educators, may books such as these make it easier to pass on your expertise and see great results.

To all parents who want the best for their children; may you exercise wisdom and patience as you implement **Riding the Wave** and blend it with many of the other wonderful things you are already doing for your children.

To the hundreds of clients who have applied this technique over the last fifteen years: I have learned from you about the ongoing benefits of this approach.

To my husband, Nico and children, Jeff, Marty and Christin – you are all the best presents anyone could wish for in life! Thank you for continuing to be there for me in so many ways.

Lastly, to my God, the ever-faithful provider of inspiration, energy and opportunity, "whose power working in all of us can do infinitely more than we can ever ask or imagine." (Ephesians 3:20)

PREFACE

The primary assumption behind *Riding the Wave* is that children with ADD or ADHD are not *out to get us* - it is more an issue of self-control. Much of the misbehavior we see in ADDers is due to their inability to focus their attention where and when it is needed. *Riding the Wave* will teach your child the cause-effect connection between their choices and the results or consequences of those choices. This is what helps to develop self-control.

The development of self-control in a child has lifelong implications. Children who learn self-control are more likely to be happier and more socially skilled as well as more self-motivated, self-confident and interested in learning.

In this handbook, I outline the steps involved in learning this powerful behavior management technique that literally saved my life and that of my child. It has proven to be effective in the lives of countless other parents and I am confident that you will see great results as well.

Dr. Teeya

Dr. Teeya Scholten, R. Psych

Calgary, Alberta, Canada
2010

FOREWORD

by Dr. Heather MacKenzie

What is self-control?

Self-control involves a lot more than just stifling your natural tendencies. It involves learning that you can manage your own time and activities. As a child growing up with ADD, I was miserable a great deal of the time and I am sure my parents were too. I had huge problems getting myself ready in the morning. I would start the routine and then the next thing I knew my parents were angry and telling me how I ruined their entire day. What happened? I guess I put on some clothes and then became interested in a book and then the world came crashing down around me. I was not trying to stir up anger or have my parents yell at me, I was just unaware of time and allowed myself to lose conscious control of the things I really needed to do. I learned on my own how to gain that self-control. I figured out that I could use the radio as my monitor in the morning. I found that, interspersed with my favorite music and chatter, the radio provided me with a reminder of the progression of time. They would announce the time every so often and that could keep me on track. I knew I had to be ready by 7:30 so I learned to leave myself a generous hour to get ready and then I would monitor my use of time via the radio. It still works to this day but I also continue to experience anxiety when I have to be ready on someone else's schedule.

Why is it important?

I truly wish I had known about self-control as a young child. It is not that I didn't know about keeping my hands to myself and being quiet in church. I knew these rules. What I really needed was an ability to understand myself and be objective about my tendencies to wander off track. I needed to become more conscious of my propensities and calmly form rules to deal with them while looking at the effect of following those rules. It would have been like taking yourself out of the eye of the storm and looking at the bigger picture. Instead, I became most concerned (and defensive) about what other people expected me to do. Those expectations often seemed arbitrary because I did not put the pieces together.

When I think about why self-control is important, there are two things that spring immediately to mind. One is that, when a child learns self-control, her parents do not have to feel like they are being pulled down by the undertow of the giant wave of impulsive and/or disruptive behavior. Family life can be smoother and more pleasant. A second issue is that, once a child learns some self-control, she will no longer feel punished for things she did not intend to do. The child with ADD often has no idea why everyone is angry or upset with her, she somehow just floated into the problem situation. Both of these things are important for day-to-day family life and the relationship between parents and children.

What is self-control like in someone with ADD?

Self-control in someone with ADD is challenging. As I pointed out above, the basic rules about hitting other people and using a quiet voice are often not all that difficult to follow. It is the things that require many different steps, occur over longer periods of time, and involve sustained attention.

Morning routines, like getting up on time, washing, brushing your teeth and dressing, that must be done within a specific time frame are difficult. Being able to accomplish all of that means that the child has to keep her attention on what she is doing while suppressing other thoughts and ideas that are much more interesting. It's not that she wants to turn up at school in her pajamas. It's often related to the fact that routine things are just not all that interesting and they take a lot of concentration.

Stopping something enjoyable in order to meet a curfew is also problematic. The adolescent with ADD simply loses track of time and, for all she knows, 30 minutes may have passed or three hours – they don't feel much different except that three hours of an enjoyable thing feels like a brief blip in time. That means, if a person with ADD has a curfew, the range of error in meeting that deadline could be several hours. That can certainly raise a parent's hackles, believe me.

Homework and other activities that require sustained attention are also very challenging. The child has this list of some rather boring stuff to do and a period of time in which to do it. After a few minutes, attention goes to other things that are more stimulating and appealing and so time passes and little homework is accomplished. The intent to finish the homework was there but not the ability to maintain attention.

What can *Riding the Wave* do?

Riding the Wave is a positive and calm way for children with ADD to learn self-control. It is fair to the child in the sense that it helps him understand clearly what the expectations are and how to abide by the rules. It avoids the many pitfalls of parenting the child with ADD. The parent is not placed in the position of a rescuer which then, ultimately, turns her into an enabler of her child with ADD. It also keeps parents from having to go to the brink of despair before trying to deal with behaviors that concern them.

Two major longer-term outcomes from using the *Riding the Wave* approach relate to the parent-child relationship and the child as an adult. *Riding the Wave* provides a process for establishing and maintaining a healthy relationship between the child and her parents. They are no longer riding the highs and lows of the child's behavior. Life feels much calmer and more enjoyable. Another important long-term benefit is that the knowledge and strategies the child learns about self-control can be applied throughout the rest of her life.

Heather MacKenzie, Ph.D.
Speech-Language Pathologist, Educator, Author, Professional Speaker
Her most recent book presents
the *Self-Regulation Program for Awareness and Resilience in Kids* (SPARK), which focuses on
teaching behavioral, cognitive, and emotional self-regulation to children.

CONTENTS

CHAPTER ONE

PARENTING A CHILD WITH ADD

It takes a lot of energy and skill to parent children, especially children with Attention Deluxe Dimension (ADD)[1]. Many parents feel like they are constantly caught in the undertow, swept beneath the torrent of their ADDer[2.] Nothing seems to work to even out life with their child with ADD. There are days when parents feel like they are riding the crest of the wave – everything seems to be fine. Then, just as suddenly, they are swept under the next wave of challenging behaviour.

If these same parents have other children, it is difficult to understand why their tried and true parenting methods just don't seem to work for their child with ADD. If the ADDer is their first, they wonder what they are doing wrong. Is it really their

> *Sometimes parenting the child with ADD seems like surfing – there are moments when you fear being caught in the undertow and other times when you are riding the crest. That is why I chose the title,* ***Riding the Wave***.

---

[1] "Attention Deluxe Dimension" is a term that I coined in 1993 to refer to ADD or AD/HD (Attention Deficit/Hyperactivity Disorder). At this point, I decided that I was no longer willing to use the terms "deficit, dysfunction or disorder" when explaining to children (or adults) how their brains work. See a free download of the book <u>Attention Deluxe Dimension: A Wholistic Approach</u> from our website www.GoodNewsAboutADD.com. The book outlines the Empowerment Plus® approach, which is a positive, balanced and effective approach to understanding and treating ADD.

[2] ADDer is a term coined by CHADD, an international organization dedicated to helping children and adults with ADD and their families. See Resources Section of this book for contact information.

fault? They don't understand why she[3] can't get ready for school in the morning. Why doesn't his homework get done? When the homework does get done, why can't it get to school? Sometimes they wonder if their in-laws, friends and neighbors are correct when they say that he just needs a little more discipline. Somehow they doubt it.

Parenting a Child with ADD

Being a good parent involves many different skills. In order to raise capable and confident adults, parents need to learn appropriate skills that work and then apply them calmly and consistently with their child.

It is the calmness and consistency that is often the greatest challenge. Many parents of children with ADD have it themselves (and may not yet know it). This makes parenting an ADDer even more challenging. Parents of ADDers often feel like remote control car drivers, steering, directing, speeding up or slowing down their child. "It's time to get up." "Time to eat." "It's time to get dressed." "Time to go to bed." "Do this." "Do that." "Don't forget this." "Don't touch that!" "Where did you put your hat, coat, homework, the dog?" Where did we go wrong? Will this ever end?

Children don't enjoy this constant badgering. Their parents don't like it either. They only do it because they don't know what else to do.

My Experience of Parenting a Child with ADD

Parenting children is a daunting responsibility for which most of us are unprepared. Many books and courses are available to help us become better parents. Those of us who have children with ADD have probably read most of these books and taken more than our fair share of parenting classes. If your family is anything like the families I typically work with, you have likely emerged from these courses feeling like a failure. I felt like this with our third child.

Our youngest child, Christin, has ADD without hyperactivity. By the time she was twelve, I was ready to tear out my hair. Whatever my husband and I had done to bring up our two sons seemed to work, but things just weren't working for our daughter. We couldn't understand it. We are both psychologists. We should have known what to do but we didn't.

---

[3] Words referring to both genders will be used alternately.

2

Christin wasn't wild and misbehaving, but she just didn't do anything without being constantly reminded. She could be very sweet and I loved her dearly, but it took an unbelievable amount of time and patience to supervise her homework. I often felt that our other two children were somewhat neglected because Christin took up so much of my time. Even then, her teachers told us she needed more attention! We tried more charts, programs and approaches for her than for our other two children combined.

Running Out of Options

By the time Christin was in Grade 6, I was exhausted. My husband, normally a very caring and nurturing person, was ready to give up. He felt that she would catch on eventually and, in the meantime, it might do her some good to suffer the consequences of not finishing her homework. "So what if she fails a grade? That might teach her to hand in her assignments." As a mother, I just couldn't allow her to experience such a major consequence. I had the feeling that she'd just keep falling through the cracks and that her self-esteem would eventually be irreparably damaged.

We pressed on. I really liked an approach to parenting where, if the child fails to do a good job at something like cleaning their room, they "owe" you some of your jobs around the house. This is in payment for the time and energy you spent chasing them. My daughter consistently owed me so much work that I had the cleanest and tidiest drawers and cupboards in town. Having to do extra household chores as well as her own chores and schoolwork left Christin feeling even more overwhelmed. We persevered, however, until one day my gentle-spirited ADDer informed me that if she ever met the author of this parenting approach, she would kill her!

The Last Failure

In desperation we started an earn-your-own-allowance chart for weekly chores. We would pay money for tasks completed and take away money for chores not done. By the end of the first week, Christin owed me $6.50. When she discovered this, she ripped up the chart and threw it in the garbage. She had definitely reached a point of total frustration and she definitely was not learning appropriate behaviour patterns.

The endless stream of botched behaviour modification attempts finally ended when I learned about the system that formed the basis for *Riding the Wave*.

Riding the Wave to the Rescue

 I decided to attend a behaviour management program[4] offered where I worked. It was for parents of children with ADD. What I learned that day changed my life and my relationship with my daughter. I was able to turn in my license as a remote control car driver who was constantly directing her actions and became a kind of guide-on-the-side, helping her learn how to direct her own actions.

We started with rules about chores. Once I had created a rule with a positive and negative consequence, Christin got to choose the time as to when the chores would be done – by 4 or 4:30 pm. The positive consequences showed her that when she chose to follow the rule and get her chores done on time, she had the freedom to do them independently. When she chose not to complete her chores on time, the negative consequence resulted in her needing supervision to complete the task. The consequence was related to the behaviour, short-term, immediate, did not involve punishment, and still ensured that the job got done. Looking back now on those years, Christin says that she remembers appreciating that the "punishment always seemed to fit the crime." With her friends, this often wasn't the case, as they seemed to be grounded for just about anything.

Although it took energy and consistent effort on my part (especially in the beginning) the results were remarkable. Within days of starting the program, we both began to experience less frustration. Christin felt encouraged and capable and I no longer felt like the bad guy or the Wicked Witch of the West.

We then worked on rules about curfews. We had a rule that we come home on time. At this point, she was going out only on the weekends. When Christin chose to come home on time, the (positive) consequence of her choice was that her curfew remained the same. When she chose not to come home on time, the (negative) consequence was that her curfew became an hour earlier the next weekend. The choices and consequences were all laid out beforehand so she was aware of the options she had. In all of her adolescent years, she was late only once and, as she is quick to remind me, "it was only by six minutes!"

---

[4] The program was a one-day workshop offered by staff to parents of children with ADD. It was excerpted from their 12-week program described in the journal article by Blakemore, Shindler and Conte (1993).

As this third edition goes to press, Christin has just graduated with a Master of Fine Arts in Film Producing from the American Film Institute (AFI) Conservatory in Los Angeles, California. She is a self-motivated and capable person with clear and positive values. She has learned to use techniques like the ones she learned in childhood to remind herself of things she has to do. She has already developed a good reputation as a Film Producer and her professors are predicting that she will be a success. Her ADD has been an advantage in dealing with the myriad details that need to be addressed on movie sets. She is happy and using her gifts. It has been a wonderful journey.

Our lovely daughter at one of her graduation ceremonies with her Pop.

CHAPTER TWO

WHAT IS *RIDING THE WAVE*?

Riding the Wave is a systematic method for learning self-control that begins with one rule and outlines the consequences if the child chooses to follow the rule or chooses not to follow the rule. The child's choice is followed by an immediate consequence, not a future reward or punishment. The approach is designed to show a clear connection between the child's choice and the consequence. It is this cause-effect connection between the choice and the consequence that teaches the kind of self-control and responsibility needed to be a successful citizen of the world.

The main features of *Riding the Wave* are that it:

- is for anyone, of any age. It has been used with children as young as two years of age, with teenagers and with young adults living away from home,

- builds self-control, internal motivation, self-monitoring and self-esteem,

- develops responsibility,

- involves clear rules with both positive and negative consequences for choices made,

- shows positive results within a short time.

Q: How is *Riding the Wave* different from other approaches?

Riding the Wave is different from typical behaviour modification methods. A star chart can be very good at getting a child's attention and can work for children who need a little extra incentive to accomplish a specific goal like reading more books.

Generally, however, a behaviour modification approach like giving out stars does not result in continued change or generalization of the learned skill to other situations. For example, the child may not continue reading books after the chart is removed. The child may also stop caring about the promised reward or threatened punishment. This leaves the adult feeling powerless to influence the child.

More than a decade ago, Deci, Koestner and Ryan (1999)[5] found that using external rewards actually reduces a person's desire, or intrinsic motivation, to do something simply for the pleasure of it. This helps to explain why typical behaviour modification programs may not work for ADDers. Giving points or stars for something the child may well care about, like helping around the house or being kind to a sibling, might actually reduce the child's willingness to do it spontaneously without a reward. This is surely not what we want for our children.

In *Riding the Wave*, there are no rewards earned nor are there any punishments levied. Even positive reinforcement in the form of comments, like "Good job!" or "Way to go!" is to be avoided. We do not want to make children reward junkies, dependent on praise from someone else. We want to encourage them to build internal images of themselves as capable of making decisions on their own. Sometimes we find it difficult not to praise our children. At first, we feel mean when we have to comment on our child's choices in a matter-of-fact way. When we realize that this is helping our child develop intrinsic motivation and self-control, we begin to understand the value of the *Riding the Wave* method.

> Using external rewards actually reduces a person's desire, or intrinsic motivation, to do something simply for the pleasure of it.

Q: How do I know if my child needs *Riding the Wave*?

If you find that your child shows any of the following characteristics and these behaviours interfere with daily life, they will likely benefit from *Riding the Wave*:

---

[5] Deci, E., Koestner, R., and Ryan, R. (1999). A Meta-Analytic Review of Experiments Examining the Effects of Extrinsic Rewards on Intrinsic Motivation. *Psychological Bulletin*, 125, pp. 627-668.

- acting first and thinking later … not looking ahead to what might happen,

- procrastinating on beginning homework or chores and then taking a long time to complete the task or not completing it satisfactorily,

- frequently losing or misplacing belongings,

- having to be reminded repeatedly to do chores, like tidying up their room or putting dirty clothes in the laundry,

- being late for school, deadlines or curfews,

- doing something only when you are *on their case*. This makes morning routines (like getting ready for school) and evening routines (like doing homework) exhausting; many parents find that they are yelling at their kids way too much.

Q: What if my spouse doesn't buy into this approach?

In typical behaviour modification programs, everyone needs to be involved. In contrast, **Riding the Wave** does not require a complete buy-in from everyone associated with the child. Throughout our daughter Christin's childhood and adolescent years, my husband, Nico, never learned the **Riding the Wave** approach. He is a kind, supportive and spontaneous kind of person but was not interested in learning this method. That meant that it was up to me to implement the program with Christin. I am saying this to encourage those of you whose partner is not interested in learning how to apply **Riding the Wave**. As with most parenting skills, it is always easier if both parents are involved, but I have seen the program work countless times with only one participating parent.

Q: How does *Riding the Wave* work?

Riding the Wave works by clarifying for the child what your expectations are in relation to a specific behaviour. Once a rule is generated, both positive and negative consequences are created that are implemented immediately after a behaviour occurs. The approach is calm, logical and positive. The negative consequences do not involve punishments but act to assist the child in following the rule. Positive consequences do not involve rewards or prizes. They help the child learn that there are positive results when they choose to follow the rules.

Q: How can I learn *Riding the Wave?*

Remember you can't jump ahead of the process. You must complete one step at a time in order for ***Riding the Wave*** to work.

If you are a parent, you can follow the step-by-step instructions in this book either by yourself or with your partner or a friend.

Complete every step before moving on to the next. The first time through, following Steps One through Ten might seem like a lot for only one behaviour, but these steps are essential building blocks. Once you and your child have learned how this method works, you can address future behaviours by just working through Steps Seven through Ten.

You can also enroll in individual sessions or a group program offered by a professional who has been trained in ***Riding the Wave***.

Contact **www.GoodNewsAboutADD.com** to find a list of professionals in your area who have training.

Q: What will I learn?

By following the steps taught in this book, you will:

- identify one behaviour of concern to focus on,

- specify what behaviour you expect,

- formulate an appropriate rule. Ideally, the rule is something that applies to the whole family. That will give a child a chance to notice whether her mother or father chooses to follow the rule. Whatever the parent expects the child to do, the parents are expected to do as well – we all have to treat each other with respect or we all need to be ready on time,

- generate both a positive and negative consequence for the child's choice of whether or not to follow the rule,

- determine what else you can do to assist the situation,

- formulate a *Back-up Plan* in case the child does not co-operate with the negative consequence.

Q: What will my child learn?

Your child will begin to exhibit increased:

- self-control,

- internal motivation,

- self-monitoring,

- responsibility,

- self-esteem.

Q: Is Riding the Wave all I need?

It is probably not all you need, but *Riding the Wave* is an essential part of a parent's tool kit. The program will help your child develop self-control which will result in him becoming a more responsible, motivated person. This, in turn, will build his self-esteem.

Q: What else will I need?

It is important to understand your child as a whole person. That means understanding his learning strengths and challenges, personality and food sensitivities. All of these aspects need to be addressed if our ADDers are to be the best they can be as naturally as possible.

Effective treatment of ADD involves looking at the whole person and all their needs. Before implementing *Riding the Wave*, I recommend that you have your child checked by their family physician or pediatrician to make sure that other factors are not interfering with the child's ability to manage their behaviour. It is also advisable to complete the **Empowerment Plus**® evaluation to identify barriers that are preventing your child from achieving his or her potential. Your child may also need help in dealing with unresolved traumas, like physical or emotional abuse, bullying, school frustrations, embarrassments or the death of a favorite aunt or pet.

Q: How effective is *Riding the Wave?*

In over fifteen years of teaching **Riding the Wave** and working with hundreds of families, I have found that no family has ever needed to address more than a few troublesome behaviours. They usually see results quickly and then, within a few months, the majority of the other behaviours of concern are eliminated, even ones that are never directly targeted. The impact generalizes to other aspects of the child's life.

Q: What if I need more assistance?

If you need more assistance in helping your child, you can contact the national offices of CHADD (Children and Adults with Attention Deficit/Hyperactivity Disorder) or the LDA (Learning Disability Association). They will help you find additional resources in your community. See the Resources Section of this book for contact information.

If you need more information or assistance in applying **Riding the Wave**, contact us at www.GoodNewsAboutADD.com. We can answer your questions and/or put you in contact with a trained professional in your area.

CHAPTER THREE

LEARNING SELF-CONTROL

Before implementing the program, it is important to make sure your child understands that the purpose of **Riding the Wave** is for them to learn self-control. You are not being mean in establishing rules and consequences but are helping your child become an independent, responsible person.

Talking with your child beforehand is done in a comfortable, enjoyable, and unemotional way. Don't be afraid to present the rule and consequences in a clear, calm, but firm manner. You have thought this through carefully and written your rule and consequences after a great deal of consideration.

The Rule

Once a rule is written, reviewed and posted, it is binding. You want the new regime to be taken seriously. For instance, if the rule is that your child does chores by a certain time and the child chooses to do the chores on time, the result is that she has had the freedom to do them independently. If she chooses not to do her chores on time, she loses the freedom to do them independently. There is no reminding, no chasing and no yelling. This will probably be a major shift in a long-standing pattern of engagement for both of you. Your new job is to check your child's choices and apply any consequences. If, for example, your child is supposed to have her chores completed by 4:30 pm, it is your job to check at exactly 4:30 to see if the chores have been completed. Your child then knows that you are serious about changing the negative patterns of complaining, chasing and/or compromising on the rules. You remain calm and state the consequence to your child's choice. If the consequence is that you will supervise her while she completes her chores, she will immediately experience the effect of her choices. There are no raised voices, no anger and no negotiation.

There may be a need for some role-playing to make sure terms, such as respectful behaviour, are understood. You can incorporate a little playfulness when doing the role-playing. Act out a behaviour and ask, "Would this be respectful behaviour?", "How about this?" "What would you say to me if I chose not to be respectful?" "What would you say if I chose to be respectful?"

The Consequences

In some behaviour modification programs, rewards are often delayed until enough points or stars are accumulated. This could mean that hours, weeks, or even months pass before the child gets his pay off. In a similar manner, negative consequences are often delayed. In *Riding the Wave*, consequences are immediate, short-term, and as natural and logical as possible. Points are not deducted nor are children threatened or prevented from participating in an activity they were looking forward to doing. We have all heard or used statements like, "If you don't behave at the mall, you can't go to Susie's birthday party next Saturday." A parent using *Riding the Wave* generates a consequence that is immediate and short-term. There is a logical relationship between the behaviour and the consequence. For example, the rule might be: "We behave at the mall. If you choose to behave at the mall, the consequence is that we can keep shopping. If you choose not to behave, you will lose the freedom to be at the mall and we will go home."

> Noticing the child's positive behaviour and pointing out the consequences of that appropriate choice is one of the most unique features of *Riding the Wave*.

The most unique, powerful and satisfying part of *Riding the Wave* is that the positive consequences are clearly stated for the child. In our society, it is typical that the squeaky wheel gets the oil. This means we usually react when things are not going well. In *Riding the Wave*, if the child chooses to follow the rule, we react. She is told that because of her choice, she has the freedom of independence. Children want to be independent. They feel capable and feeling capable builds their self-esteem.

Cause-Effect Connection between Rules and Consequences

Through this approach, your child takes control of whether she will experience a positive or negative consequence. She knows beforehand what the rule is and what the consequences are so she can make a choice. This is a *cause-effect* connection. The *cause* is her choice and the *effect* is the consequence of that choice.

When your child learns this cause-effect relationship, self-control is developed and applied to other parts of his life. This is what we call *generalization*: the effects of using this technique generalizes it to other situations.

Dakota's Story

Recently one of my very active five-year-old clients learned that if he chose to keep his attention on his soccer game and not wander off the field, the consequence was that he would have the freedom to keep playing. If not, his parents would take him home. At his next soccer game he chose not to stay with the team and he lost the freedom to stay.

He screamed and cried all the way home.

However, at the soccer games that followed, Dakota was much more focused and stayed with the team. His parents were truly shocked when they noticed that Dakota began following routines at school as well. They couldn't believe how quickly his self-control and ability to focus had generalized from the soccer game to other settings.

Keeping the Momentum

After implementing **Riding the Wave**, parents learn to use the language of choice and consequence in other situations and at other times. They become more skillful at noticing their child's choices when he is following the rules rather than just noticing when he isn't. Parents are advised to aim for three positive comments for every negative one. If you focus on the positives, the method will be more effective and you will see results faster.

I often use the analogy of juggling plates on a pole. In the beginning, the juggler needs to spin the plates frequently to maintain momentum. Once the plates are spinning nicely, she only needs to give them a nudge in the right direction every now and then. This is the case with ***Riding the Wave***. In the beginning, you need to be vigilant and consistent, noticing your child's choices continually. Once the behaviour has changed (for example, your child is getting ready for school on time, doing his chores or being respectful to others) you keep up the momentum by noticing his choices and commenting about the positive results.

Byron's Story - A Case Study

Fifteen-year-old Byron was the middle child in a family of three children, all of whom had learning discrepancies. His siblings had progressed well, but Byron was floundering.

Since he had been considered moody from early childhood, we suspected sensitivity to wheat in his diet. He was willing to eliminate wheat from his diet and, once it was removed, his mood became much more pleasant and stable. He appreciated feeling better and said that his head no longer felt "so tired all the time."

He also had a VSLD (Visual-Spatial Learning Discrepancy), which meant that he had a difficult time writing neatly and putting his ideas on paper. We suggested that he begin to do his written work on a computer and this reduced his feelings of frustration considerably.

His ENFP (Extraverted-iNtuiting-Feeling-Perceiving) personality type meant that he was a talkative person who would rather gather new information than sit down to do an assignment or finish a project in which he wasn't interested. He was an innovative person for whom detail work was a real challenge. Proof-reading was an activity to be avoided at all costs! A fellow student was enlisted for help with proof-reading, while Byron's skills in brainstorming were engaged when other students needed help coming up with ideas.

Byron had been diagnosed earlier with ADHD and had been put on medication. He experienced side-effects such as a reduced appetite which suggested that the dose was too high. His medication was adjusted to a smaller amount. There were still serious concerns, however. In school his teacher would typically explain the assignment to the class and check with Byron to be sure that he understood what he had to do. As long as the teacher was close by, Byron would work. As soon as she walked away, he would stop working and begin to fool around with his classmates. This pattern had been going on for years but, now that he was in high school, his behaviour was becoming increasingly disruptive in school. He was often disrespectful to his parents and he was beginning to use drugs.

After a basic **Empowerment Plus**® evaluation, his parents decided to learn ***Riding the Wave.***

His parents wanted to immediately work on his lack of respect, drug use and school work, but they understood that, in the beginning, they needed to choose a behaviour that was lower on their list of priorities. In this way, they could be calmer and more objective in implementing the rules.

His parents chose to work on getting Byron to do his chores on time. When I asked what his chores were, his mother gave a different list than his father. If they weren't clear on what his duties were, how could Byron be expected to know what had to be done?

Once the chore list was clarified, the rule and consequences were established. His daily chores were walking, feeding, and cleaning up after the dog.

Their first rule was as follows:

Rule: We do our chores on time. (For Byron, this was defined as every day by 5 pm.)

Positive consequence (+): If you choose to complete your chores on time, you will have had the freedom to do them independently.

Negative consequence (-): If you choose not to complete your chores on time, you will lose the freedom to do them independently. We will supervise you and tell you what order to do them in and how to do them.

Then the parents created their script, laminated one copy to keep in their pockets, and posted another copy on the inside of the kitchen cupboard door. Their script was as follows:

(+) *"Byron, I notice that you chose to do your chores on time, as a result you have had the freedom to do them independently."*

OR

(-) *"Byron, I notice that you have chosen not to do your chores on time. As a result, you have lost the freedom to do them independently. I will supervise you. Let's go."*

Byron's parents explained that the purpose of ***Riding the Wave*** was to teach Byron self-control and to get them off his back in terms of nagging. They told him that in life we have rules. If we choose to follow the rules, we generally have a lot of freedom. If not, we lose freedom. They used the example of following the rules of the road while driving. If someone chooses to follow the rules, such as driving within the speed limit, the consequence is that they are free to keep their license. If they choose not to follow the rules of the road and they are caught, they have to pay a fine and possibly lose their license and the freedom to drive for a while. Byron understood this concept but was not really impressed with the idea of having to do his chores by a particular time. He said that he didn't care if his parents told him what to do. They were already harassing him about it, so what was the difference?

The parents then explained that this was a different way to do things. If he chose not to do his chores on time, he was expected to co-operate when his parents supervised him while he finished them. That meant that he needed to do exactly as they said, without resisting, commenting, or complaining.

Byron was then told the Back-up Plan.

The rule was: "We co-operate with the negative consequence."

+ If you choose to co-operate with the negative consequence, the result is that it is over quickly and you can go about your life.

- If you choose not to co-operate with the negative consequence, the result is that it is not over quickly and you lose your freedom for the rest of the evening. That means no contact with friends, no TV, no computer and no video games.

They suggested role-playing what it would look like to be co-operative and not co-operative, but Byron didn't want to participate. The parents decided to role-play these various options with each other. As soon as Byron saw them doing this, he decided to get in on the action and wanted to role-play his parents. It was interesting for his parents to see how Byron acted out their roles. It gave them a glimpse of how they came across to him and they decided that they were not being very respectful at times. At the end of the preparation session, they were all having fun and felt ready to see what would happen with this new method.

At first, there was supervision every night, but by the third day Byron began to remember to do his chores. It was hard for his Mom not to remind him as 5 pm approached, but she was able to wait until the deadline arrived. She was thrilled when Byron chose to do his chores on time without being reminded.

After a few three weeks of implementing **Riding the Wave**, Byron said to his mother, "I think I'm becoming more responsible, don't you?" It was music to her ears!

The next behaviour they targeted was treating each other with respect. This worked like a charm and the atmosphere in the house greatly improved. His mother reported that Byron's self-esteem, confidence, and willingness to get his school work done had also greatly improved.

Since Byron was continuing to use marijuana, the parents decided to refer Byron to a program that dealt directly with drug issues. The last time I saw this family, Byron was in treatment for this.

CHAPTER FOUR

AN OVERVIEW OF THE TEN STEPS

In this chapter the ten steps to success are presented. Remember that every step must be followed in order to get the desired results. Time estimates to complete each step are provided in the next chapter. They are rough guidelines only. Your situation is unique and may take more or less time.

THE TEN STEPS

Step One: Identify all of your child's behaviours that concern you.

Step Two: Figure out when, where, and at what time of day these behaviours occur.

Step Three: Re-organize your list of behaviours in priority, from the most to the least bothersome. If you're working with a spouse or partner, you will put your ideas together to create a shared list of behaviours of concern. Remember: your child is not involved in your discussions of his behaviours that concern you. Hearing you talk about all of the things that bother you about him could cause some serious damage to your relationship with him and could erode his confidence and self-esteem.

Step Four: Take a step back and think about what you like about your child and in what ways you are a good parent. It's important to remember these things when you are in the throes of dealing with negative behaviour.

Step Five: Observe your child and watch what he does and how you respond. You decide if the way he behaves are things you'd like to see repeated (positive) or not (negative). You also make a note of how you responded. When most parents do this exercise they realize how levels of fatigue or time pressure contribute to being much less patient with their child than they would like to be.

Step Six: Select a behaviour from your list that will be targeted. The behaviour you select is one of those you decided was a lower priority. This is done so that the first time through **Riding the Wave** focuses on a behaviour that has less emotion riding on it. It makes it easier to remain calm, more objective and likely more successful. You and your child are learning how to use this approach and it's much easier to do it with a behaviour that is not highly charged with emotion. Once you have learned the techniques, you can target any behaviour you choose.

Step Seven: Complete the *Behaviour Management Worksheet*. You will need to think carefully about what behaviour you expect from your child, what the family rule will be, what the positive and negative consequences are and a Back-up Plan if your child chooses not to comply with the negative consequence. Every single loophole has to be addressed at this point.

Step Eight: Create and practice your own personalized script. You need to make sure that you are using the correct words. The key phrases are: "I notice that you *chose…*" and "The *consequence* is…." Use of the words, *chose* and *consequence,* are what makes the cause-effect connection clear for your child and this, in turn, builds self-control.

Step Nine: Step Nine has to be done *every time* you focus on a new behaviour of concern. It involves explaining the rules and consequences to your child and why you are doing this. You are also making sure that everyone understands what is expected and that your child has the necessary skills/tools to perform the task. Role-playing can be helpful, fun and enlightening.

Step Ten: You are now ready to implement the rule. You must use precision in your language, restraint in not reminding and constraint in praising your child's efforts. It takes active effort to remember when you are supposed to notice his choices. If chores are to be done by 5 pm, you will need to notice his choices precisely at that time: *"I notice that you chose to walk the dog on time. As a result you have had the freedom to do it independently."* We don't usually talk to each other this way but it helps confirm the cause-effect connection and is part of the distinctiveness of the **Riding the Wave** approach.

CHAPTER FIVE

THE TEN STEPS TO SUCCESS

STEP ONE – Write down at least ten of your child's behaviours that concern you.

Time estimate: 15 min.

Directions: Use the *Behaviours of Concern* Form at the back of this book. Both parents make up their own separate list. Fill in the left column with behaviours you wish would disappear or change. Do not worry about the order in which you write the behaviours. Be descriptive, specific, and objective. Tell exactly what happens. Try not to be judgmental; just describe what your child does. For instance, use *interrupts conversations* instead of writing *he is rude*. Write *rips up papers when angry* instead of *is destructive*. Describe the behaviour in such a way that someone else could picture exactly what your child is doing by just reading your words.

The Behaviours of Concern Form

Behaviours of Concern	Situation (when and where and what time of day the behaviour occurs)
Does not start homework on his own	
Interrupts conversations	
Rips up belongings of others	
Doesn't take out the garbage on his own	
Hits his brothers	
Complains	
Forgets to bring home homework	
Doesn't get ready in the morning without reminding	
Doesn't hang up his towel	
Doesn't remember to feed the dog	

STEP TWO – Describe the situation in which each behaviour typically occurs.

Time estimate: 10 minutes

Directions: In the right column of the *Behaviours of Concern* Form, describe when, where and what time of day the behaviour of concern typically occurs. You may discover that certain problems occur at specific times, such as when you and/or your child are tired, when he just arrives home from school or when you just come home from work. This may be new information that you can use in understanding you and your child better.

Cross off any behaviours that are strong habits, such as thumb sucking, because they can be dealt with later when the method has been learned. Cross off anything that is a problem for you but is not detrimental to your child's health or well-being, such as wearing socks that don't match or not eating everything on their plate.

Behaviours of Concern - The Situation

Behaviours of Concern	Situation (when and where and what time of day the behaviour occurs)
Does not start homework on his own	*After school, when it's homework time (4 to 5 pm)*
Interrupts conversations	*When anyone else is talking and he thinks of something to say*
Rips up belongings of others	*When angry that he can't have or do something he wants, especially when told to turn off his video game*
Doesn't take out the garbage on his own	*Garbage days before school*
Hits his brothers	*When they bother him*
Complains	*When we ask him to do something he doesn't like*
Forgets to bring home homework	*Most days*
Doesn't get ready in the morning without reminding	*Every day except weekends*
Doesn't hang up his towel	*After his shower*
Doesn't remember to feed the dog	*Every day*

STEP THREE – Arrange the behaviours of concern in their order of priority.

Time estimate: 10 minutes

Directions: Now that you have a list of at least ten behaviours, cut up the Behaviours of Concern Form so that each behaviour is now on a separate slip of paper. Arrange them from *Most to Least Bothersome* - that is, which behaviours get to you most and which don't bother you as much. Focus on the behaviour itself, not how often it occurs. Some parents put a behaviour, like lying or stealing, on the bottom half of the list because it might not be happening very often. This is not correct. The behaviour of lying or stealing is usually one that bothers parents a lot so it should go near the top of the list, no matter how infrequently it actually occurs.

Once you have arranged the behaviours in order, take a blank piece of paper and arrange the behaviours vertically with the most bothersome at the top and the least bothersome at the bottom. Tape the strips onto the new page using a single, long piece of clear tape placed down the center of the page.

Note: If you are learning the method with a partner, share your list of behaviours of concern with your partner. Then cut up both lists and place them in an order on which you can both agree. Then tape the behaviours on a new page in their order of priority. Some compromise may be necessary at this point. If you have a lot of behaviours of concern you may need two papers taped together to make a very long sheet.

Behaviours of Concern arranged in order of priority

Behaviour of Concern	Situation (when and where and what time of day the behaviour occurs)
MOST BOTHERSOME	
Rips up belongings of others	*When angry that he can't have or do something he wants, especially when told to turn off his video game*

Hits his brothers	*When they bother him*
Complains	*When we ask him to do something he doesn't like*
Forgets to bring home homework	*Most days*
Doesn't get ready in the morning without reminding	*Every day except weekends*
Does not start homework on his own	*After school, when it's homework time (4 to 5 pm)*
Doesn't put away his toys	*Every day*
Interrupts conversations	*When anyone else is talking and he thinks of something to say*
Doesn't take out the garbage without reminding	*Garbage days before school*
Doesn't hang up his towel	*After his shower*
LEAST BOTHERSOME	

STEP FOUR – Think about what you like about your child and ways that you are a good parent.

Time estimate: 10 minutes

Directions: Use the *Things I like about My Child and Ways I am a Good Parent* Form. Take time to list at least three things in each area. An example is shown opposite.

Things I Like about My Child and Ways I am a Good Parent

Things I like about my child
Good sense of humor
Creative
Friendly
Ways I am a good parent
Provide nourishment
Drive him to soccer games
Encourage him to have friends over

Do not proceed to Step Five until you have completed this exercise. This step may not seem especially important but it is part of the basic building blocks that is necessary to the success of the *Riding the Wave* approach. If you and your partner are learning this method together, be sure to fill out your own lists and then share them.

STEP FIVE – Responses to My Child's Behaviour.

This step has two parts. Part 1 involves observing yourself with your child. Part 2 is analyzing the results to decide if this was a typical example of your interactions.

Step Five - Part 1 – Observing Yourself and Your Child

Time estimate: 60 minutes

Directions: Use the *Responding to My Child's Behaviour* Form at the back of this book. The purpose of this exercise is to give you practice identifying both positive and negative behaviours and monitoring how you respond to your child. Pick an hour all at once or in four fifteen-minute segments to observe your interactions. Take your time and write down exactly what your child does and how you respond. If your child does something you would like to see repeated, write this down in the Positive Behaviours column. Write down how you responded to this positive behaviour. If your child does something that you would not like to see repeated, write it down in the Negative Behaviours column. Write down how you responded to the negative behaviour. See the example below about several Parent-Child interactions that occurred during a one-hour time frame on a school night.

Responding to My Child's Behaviour

Positive Behaviours		Negative Behaviours	
What's working now?		*What's not working yet?*	
What did my child do?	*How did I respond?*	*What did my child do?*	*How did I respond?*
Played nicely with his brother	Smiled at him	Interrupted me when I was talking to my husband	I frowned at him
Took out the garbage when I asked him to	Said "Thank you"	Lied about not having homework	I told him that I was fed up with his behaviour
		Threw his brother's baseball mitt when I told him I wouldn't take him to the mall	I grabbed the mitt and sent him to his room

Is this a typical sample of my interaction with my child? _____

Step Five - Part 2 - Analyzing the results

Time estimate: 5 minutes

Directions: After you have completed the *Responding to My Child's Behaviour* Form, take some time to think about the results. Is this a typical sample of your interactions with your child? If no, what is usually different? Did you see any patterns? For instance, does your child seem to get angry more often just before meals or when he is tired or when it's time to do school work? Do you seem to lose your cool more often when you are tired or stressed? Do you actually notice the positives? Do you comment on these at all? How? What have you learned about yourself during this exercise?

Rachel's Story

Years ago, I was teaching ***Riding the Wave*** to the father of a highly intelligent 25-year-old who was barely able to function independently. When the father noted his interactions with his daughter, he found that he only responded to Rachel when she did something inappropriate. When I asked why he did not say anything when she did something positive, he said that she should know all this by now. It was an eye opener for him when he realized that Rachel was getting a lot of attention for being incompetent. He needed to respond differently if she was going to improve.

Parenting the child with ADD sometimes seems like surfing – it takes a lot of skill but also careful balance and forward movement

STEP SIX – Choose a behaviour to work on with your child.

Time estimate: 5 minutes

Directions: Choose a behaviour to work on with your child by using the list you created in Step Three. This is the list with the behaviours arranged in order from *Most Bothersome Behaviours* at the top to the *Least Bothersome* at the bottom. If you are working with a partner, use your combined list. Count all the behaviours and draw a horizontal line across the page that divides the list into halves. For example, if you have ten *Behaviours of Concern,* draw a line under Behaviour #5 on the list. Now select a behaviour to work on which is on the bottom half of the list. Write down the behaviour you have selected on the *Behaviour Management Worksheet* found at the back of this book.

How to Select Target Behaviour

MOST BOTHERSOME	
Rips up belongings of others	When angry that he can't have or do something he wants, especially when told to turn off his video game
Hits his brothers	When they bother him
Complains	When we ask him to do something he doesn't like
Forgets to bring home homework	Most days
Doesn't get ready in the morning without reminding	Every day except weekends

Does not start homework on his own	After school, when it's homework time (4 to 5 pm)
Doesn't put away his toys	Every day
Interrupts conversations	When anyone else is talking and he thinks of something to say
Doesn't take out the garbage without reminding	Garbage days before school
Doesn't hang up his towel	After his shower
LEAST BOTHERSOME	

Here are some commonly asked Questions and Answers about Step Six:

Q: What good can it do to start with only one behaviour?

Starting off with only one behaviour allows everyone to learn how to use the ***Riding the Wave*** approach. It also helps your child learn about making choices. He will quickly discover that this new approach is clear and straightforward and that he has control about whether the outcome of his behaviour is positive or negative. You will discover how it feels to remain calm and objective and how to allow your child the freedom to decide whether he wishes to follow the rules or not.

If you start off slowly but consistently, it is remarkable how quickly you will see results. Often, just focusing on one behaviour has an effect on other behaviours; learning in one situation generalizes to another situation without direct teaching. We call this the *ripple effect*. It occurs because your child is learning self-control and will begin to use it in other behaviours where needed. For example, once your child learns how to do get ready for school in the morning, it's likely that she will be able to use the same skills to get ready for bed in the evening. In many cases, behaviours that parents were originally concerned about become resolved without direct intervention.

When I teach this program to parents, it is my experience that both parents and children see results within ten days of applying the rule and consequences. Remember that ***Riding the Wave*** is one more tool in your toolbox for helping your child to be the best he can be as naturally as possible.

Q: Why choose something from the bottom half of the list when my major concerns are on the top?

During the process of learning the technique, it is much easier if you are focusing on a behaviour that doesn't send you through the roof. The behaviours on the bottom half of the list tends to have less emotional baggage connected to them. You can be more objective and detached about it. You won't have the *I'm-going-to-explode-if-he-does-it-one-more-time* feeling. Also, you and your child are more likely to see changes quickly when you choose a behaviour that is less problematic.

Q: What if my child is too young to understand the word consequence?

Many parents have found that, when they explain the concept of cause and effect, even small children are able to understand what a consequence is. You might help him understand by using everyday examples. For example, you could explain, "When you eat breakfast, the result or consequence is that you are not hungry anymore." or "When you throw a ball in the air, the consequence is that it goes up." You can substitute the word "result" for "consequence" if you are more comfortable with that term.

Q: What if I'd really like to see a change in a certain behaviour, but I don't believe that it can realistically be changed?

Even if you don't feel hopeful that you can do anything about it, select that behaviour and follow all the steps consistently. Remember to choose any behaviour you wish to work on as long as it is from the bottom half of the list on your first time through the ***Riding the Wave*** approach. If you want to focus on a behaviour that is on the top half of the list, wait until you have had success in a behaviour that is not as emotionally charged. If a behaviour is particularly destructive or if you are concerned for the safety of your child, it is important to immediately seek professional help by contacting your family physician, pediatrician or by calling your local emergency number.

STEP SEVEN – Complete the Behaviour Management Worksheet.

Time estimate: 1–2 hours the first time through; 5-10 minutes for addressing subsequent behaviours.

Directions: Completing the *Behaviour Management Worksheet* is the most important step in the entire **Riding the Wave** method. It is also the most time-consuming. The more thoroughly you complete the worksheet, the easier the remainder of the steps will be.

Use the *Behaviour Management Worksheet* found at the back of this book. An example is shown opposite.

Think carefully about what you expect of your child, how this can be turned into a rule that applies to the whole family and what consequences you might choose. The rule and your expectations must be clear and consistent. You also need to be able and willing to implement the consequences. Every potential loophole must be considered. Remember: there will be no more reminding your child of the rules so consistency is needed if the child is expected to remember what she is expected to do.

Behaviour Management Worksheet

Selected behaviour of concern *What is the unacceptable behaviour?*

Expected behaviour *What do you expect the child to do?*

Rule *State the rule in a positive manner, describing what is expected. If possible, the rule should apply to the whole family.*

Consequences *Include things that can be done immediately, do not take a lot of time and that flow naturally or logically from the expected behaviour.*

Positive (+) _____

Negative (-) _____

Script *What will you actually say to your child?*

(+) *(Name of child), I notice that you have chosen to (state the rule). As a result, you have had the freedom to...*

(-) *(Name of child), I notice that you have chosen <u>not</u> to (state the rule). As a result, you have lost the freedom to...*

What else can I do to help the situation? *Sometimes making up charts of daily schedules or checklists of activities or chores can help make your expectations clearer. It saves you from having to remind your child and provides a ready reference guide for him/her.*

Back-up Plan *You need to decide ahead of time what you will do if your child refuses to comply with the negative consequence. This is important to have in place in order to be ready for anything.*

Rule

The Back-up Plan Rule is always: We co-operate with the negative consequence.

(+) If your child chooses to co-operate, the consequence is that it is over quickly and she can go on with her life.

(-) If your child chooses not to co-operate, the consequence is that it is not over quickly and she loses the freedom to go on with life in the normal way for the rest of the day. She might lose freedom to watch TV or play videogames or go over to her friend's house, for example.

Select behaviour of concern. Decide what the behaviour of concern is. I was recently working with a couple with a twenty-year-old daughter. Farhana attended school, had a part-time job and always seemed to be running out the door late for her next activity. She also loved to cook at all times of the day and night but rarely cleaned up after she was finished. When we first completed the *Behaviour Management Worksheet*, Farhana's parents selected cleaning up after cooking as their Behaviour of Concern.

Specify expected behaviour. Once you have chosen a behaviour of concern, write a clear description of what behaviour you expect from your child instead of the behaviour of concern. We always explain what we want to see, rather than what we don't want to see. Stating the expected behaviour in positive terms helps the child remember what to do rather than what not to do. State a rule for her to follow using positive and straightforward words that describe what is expected.

Generate a rule. Ideally you should generate a rule that applies to the whole family. Examples of these rules would be: *"We treat each other with respect." "We get ready on time." "We take care of our belongings."* Farhana's parents chose the rule: *"We clean up after ourselves."*

Determine the positive consequence. In choosing consequences, I find the concepts of freedom and independence useful when considering possible consequences. For example, a consequence could be: *"You will have the freedom to get ready on your own."*

Once you have determined the behaviour you are going to target, it can be helpful to refer to the *Chart of Examples of Behaviours, Rules and Consequen*ces found in the Appendix to give you an idea of the types of rules and consequences that other people have used. Most of us have never actually identified the positive consequence of choosing to follow certain rules of society. Who ever thinks that because I chose to stop at the stop sign, the consequence is that I can keep my license? Nevertheless, this <u>is</u> really the positive consequence. In ***Riding the Wave***, we are making these positive consequences obvious.

Determine the negative consequence. Consequences must be immediate and short-term. Consequences need to be applied right away and be over within five minutes or a day at most. Eventually, your child will be saying to himself, "I chose to do this and the result was that. Hmmm, I'd better think carefully next time about what I choose to do." This close connection between cause and effect makes the learning much easier.

When she chose not to clean up the kitchen after she finished cooking, the consequence for Farhana was that she lost the freedom to clean up on her own.

Consequences must be natural, logical and non-punitive. Consequences need to be connected with the negative behaviour in some way. For example, if the rule is that the child must play quietly when in the house, the consequence if he chooses not to play quietly might be losing the freedom to be in the house for five minutes. An unnatural consequence would be that the child would lose ten minutes of TV time or would not be allowed to go to Grandma's this weekend. These are threats and punishments not directly connected to the rule. Even the old-fashioned threat of "wait till your Father gets home!" is too late and not directly connected to the rule.

You must be able to implement the negative consequence. A consequence of never having your allowance again is not realistic, although it can be tempting to say this, especially when frustrated. Grounding a child for two weeks is another poorly selected consequence. It is not immediate enough and having a teenager mope around the house for two weeks is often more of a punishment for the family than for a moody adolescent.

When Farhana's parents began to implement the rule about cleaning the kitchen and the consequences, they discovered that they were rarely home (or were in bed asleep) when she finished cooking. That meant they couldn't implement the consequence. We then had to refine the rule and consequence. The rule became a job assignment for Farhana to clean up the kitchen every night by 10:30 pm. If she chose to clean up the kitchen by 10:30 pm, the consequence was that she had the freedom to do it on her own. If not, she lost the freedom to do it on her own and one of her parents would supervise her. It took quite a bit of negotiation between the parents to come up with a strategy for handling any mess that she left during the day, but we finally worked out something that was clear and comfortable for both parents: any dishes their daughter left out during the day would be put into a plastic bin and stored out of everyone else's way. They also decided that there would be no cooking after 10:30 pm. Sometimes parents need to be encouraged to stand up for themselves, realizing that it is their house and they have a right to set rules with parameters that are fair to everyone.

> Because the consequences in *Riding the Wave* are clear, consistent and worked out ahead of time, they are usually a relief to all parties involved.

What else can you do? Once you have generated the rule and consequences, it is time to get input from your child. You can ask, "Do you want the final clean-up time to be 10 or 10:30 pm?" or "Do you want your morning alarm to go off at 7 or 7:30 am?" This gives the child ownership while staying true to the original rule and consequences. Children are often very good at suggesting consequences, although, in my experience, they tend to be much harder on themselves than we would be!

Next, think about things that might help your child follow the rule. Schedules, checklists, and clearer indications of expectations can be helpful.

Develop a *Back-up Plan*. Always develop a *Back-up Plan* in case your child chooses not to co-operate with the negative consequences on the *Behaviour Management Worksheet*. Some parents are worried that their child will object to doing whatever is required. This is where the preparation work is crucial. It is important to explain the *Back-up Plan* to your child before implementing the rule. If your child is generally co-operative, you may only need to notice by commenting on his choice to co-operate and the positive consequence the first few times and then once every few weeks. If your child tends not to be co-operative, it is essential that you remain calm, firm, and take a no-nonsense approach. This is not a time for cajoling, talking with each other, getting backrubs or negotiating. It is time to simply implement the negative consequence.

You will have to decide what lack of co-operation looks like. Is she allowed to say anything at all? It might be okay for her to give a respectful I-message telling how she feels like, "I feel so frustrated that I didn't make the deadline." Do you expect silent compliance? This is not a time for a discussion about her feelings or any negotiation; it is time to get the job done. Self-discipline will be needed on your part here. There should be no talking about anything except what has to be done next. Feelings can be discussed later. Is a groan allowed or rolling of the eyes as long as she carries out your commands quickly? It's your decision; but whatever you decide needs to be honored by you as well as her. You may feel mean but I would encourage you to realize that you are being predictable and consistent and that you are really teaching her that her choices have consequences. Every time you follow through, it is money in your child's bank of self-control, internal motivation, self-monitoring, responsibility and self-esteem.

Prior to implementing the plan, it can be helpful to take turns role-playing the family rule and the *Back-up Plan* to make sure that your child understands what is expected and what will happen. It can actually be fun and enlightening to playfully take turns being the adult and child in the situation.

An example of one family's *Behaviour Management Worksheet* is shown below along with a discussion of the decision-making process they used.

The Decision-Making Process

> **Selected behaviour of concern** *Mark does not put away his toys*

> **Expected behaviour** *I expect Mark to put away his toys by 7 pm.*

> **Rule** *We tidy up after ourselves. (Mark's toys need to be put away by 7 pm.)*

The words in the rule showed that it applies to the whole family. We all tidy up after ourselves. However, in seven-year-old Mark's case, there is a deadline of 7 pm.

Every family is different and your situation is unique so there is no right and wrong in terms of what you are expecting. It is only important that the rule be crystal clear to everyone involved, realistic, and enforceable. You have to have the energy to supervise what you are requesting be done.

Here are some things that need to be decided:

1. Which time piece will be the reference for determining when it is exactly 7 pm? Which clock or whose watch? If there is a loophole your child will find it. It's easy to imagine your child saying, "Look, it's not 7:00 on the kitchen clock, it is only 6:57. I still have three minutes to do my job!" In this example, we decided to use the clock on the kitchen oven.

2. What do you mean by *tidying up*? Do you mean tidy up his toys only or his clothes? What about shoes, boots, towels, toothbrushes, dishes or homework papers? Only his belongings or everyone else's too? Which rooms need to be tidied - the family room, the washroom, his bedroom or the entire house or apartment? In this case, we decided to have Mark tidy up his own belongings in every room in the house except his bedroom (i.e., playroom, living room, dining room, kitchen, bathroom and front hall). Toys and other belongings could be put in his bedroom, but not on the floor. We planned to address the bedroom in another rule to be learned and applied later.

3. How is Mark going to know when it is time to start cleaning up? If he can tell time on his own, he is responsible for noticing it. In this case, you are off the hook. If he is not yet telling time on his own, you might ask him how long he thinks he might need for the activity of tidying up. If he says half an hour, you can ask if he would like to be told when it is 6:30. If he says "Yes" he'd like to be told the time, then your job as the parent is simply to act like a talking clock and say "It is 6:30." You do

not say, "It is 6:30. What do you have to do?" or "It's 6:30 now. Time to tidy up!" There is no reminding in **Riding the Wave**. We want every child to learn to rely on himself rather than external monitoring by his parents. If he doesn't want to be told the time, then you can ask how he will know when the deadline is. You could show him where the hands on the clock will be when it is 6:30 and see what happens.

4. Do you expect this tidying up to be done every day or does he get a day off? What if you are out or he is not home until after 7 pm? It should be a stand-alone rule as much as possible. Do you want to have a rule that his tidying has to be done within half an hour of arriving home? A lot will depend on your circumstances, your preferences and the age of your child. If you have a teenager who likes to play at a friend's house after school and/or who sometimes stays for supper, you will want to clarify what will happen in these cases. Will he decide to tidy up before he leaves in the morning so that his job will be done by 7 pm or will he have to come home before 7 pm, tidy up and go back out? It's up to you to figure it out first and then to get your child's input when you are making your final decisions about how the rule will look.

In Mark's case, they decided that the rule would hold for every day. They weren't willing to have the house a mess at the end of any day of the week. They also decided that if they weren't going to be home in time for him to tidy up by 7 pm, the secondary rule would be that he'd have to tidy up within half an hour of them arriving home. It was their job as parents to make sure that they actually came home early enough to leave time for tidy up. As soon as they arrived home, they would set the buzzer on the kitchen stove and tell Mark that it would ring in half an hour. If they knew they might be out very late, the deadline would become 5 instead of 7 pm and they would tell Mark by noon on that day at the latest, so he would have plenty of time to decide when he wanted to tidy up. See the family's personalized script in Step Eight.

Consequences

Positive (+) *You have the freedom to do it independently.*

All of your toys need to be off the playroom floor and put into the toy box. All of your clothes or other belongings in the playroom, front hall, living room, kitchen, family room and bathroom need to be put away where they belong. All of the clothes in your room hung up in the cupboard, or placed on your chair, or in the dirty clothes hamper. School supplies and homework on your desk. Nothing can be left on the floor in any of these rooms.

Negative (-) *You will lose the freedom to do it on your own. Let's go.* (I will supervise you, tell you where to put things and in what order.)

Script

(+) *Mark, I notice that you chose to tidy up after yourself. As a result, you have had the freedom to do it independently.*

(-) *Mark, I notice that you chose <u>not</u> to tidy up after yourself. As a result, you have lost the freedom to do it independently.*

What else can I do to help the situation?

Since Mark wanted to be told when it was 6:30 pm, his mother set her watch to go off at 6:30 pm so she could tell him the time. She would set it again for 7 pm so she could notice his choice and determine the consequence. This was a fair, precise, and consistent way to help the parents remember to notice what Mark had done at the specified time.

The parents made up a chart to go on the cupboard door and in Mark's bedroom reminding him of the rooms that needed to be tidied and what needed to be done. Rooms to be tided: playroom, front hall, living room, kitchen, family room and bathroom. Actions to be taken: All toys in toy box and other belongings where they go, including toothbrush in holder, toothpaste in drawer, towels on racks, shoes in hall cupboard, clean clothes hung up or put on chair, dirty clothes in hamper, and school work on desk. Everything to be off the floor in every room.

Back-up Plan

The Back-up Plan rule is: We co-operate with any negative consequences.

+ If you choose to co-operate with the negative consequence, it is over right away and you can get on with your life.

- If you choose not to co-operate with the negative consequence, it is not over right away and you lose the freedom to get on with your life. (There will be no access to TV, computer or videogames for the rest of the day.)

STEP EIGHT – Create your own personalized script.

Time estimate: 20 minutes

Directions: Write out exactly what you will say to your child. This gives you practice in streamlining your communication while making sure that you include the important words about choice and consequence.

It often helps to post the rule and the consequences somewhere that is easily accessible, such as on the inside of a kitchen cupboard door. Being placed on the inside of a door protects your child's privacy when friends are over but still makes it easily accessible for you to refer to. Some parents type out the actual words they will use, laminate the page and keep it in their pockets for ready reference. They find that this helps them become familiar with the wording and serves as a reminder to catch their child making choices that have positive results instead of just the ones that have negative results.

You do not have to be creative in your wording. In fact, it is better to repeat the script word-for-word. You will feel and sound like a robot at times and your children may groan when they hear you saying the exact phrase over and over again. However, clear, consistent wording gets into their heads and when they start to hear three positive comments to every negative one it will be like depositing money in their self-esteem-building bank. You will find that it feels much better noticing and saying positive things to your child instead of constantly criticizing and chasing him to do what he has neglected to do.

Example Script

Rule *We tidy up after ourselves. (Everyday by 7 pm on the kitchen clock, or by 5 pm if we are going out later in the day or within half an hour of arriving home if we are delayed in coming home.)*
Consequences   **Positive (+)** *Freedom to do it independently*   **Negative (-)** *Lose freedom to do it independently*
Script   **(+)** *Mark, I notice that you chose to tidy up after yourself; the consequence is that you have had the freedom to do it independently.*   **(-)** *Mark, I notice that you chose not to tidy up after yourself; the consequence is that you have lost the freedom to do it on your own. Let's go.*
Back-up Plan   **Rule** *We co-operate with the negative consequence.*   **Consequences**   **Positive (+)** *Mark, I notice that you chose to co-operate with the negative consequence. As a result, it is over right away and you can get on with your life.*   **Negative (-)** *Mark, I notice that you chose not to co-operate with the negative consequence. As a result, it is not over right away and you have lost the freedom to get on with your life. Once you have done what you were supposed to do, there will be no more access to TV, computer or videogames for the rest of the day.*

STEP NINE – Explain the method, the rule and the consequences to your child and to the rest of the family.

Time estimate: 30 minutes (for first behaviour only); 5-10 minutes (for every subsequent rule and consequences).

Directions: Before you implement the very first rule, it is essential to explain fully to your child what will be happening and why you are doing this. Do it in a relaxed, comfortable, fun-filled way. Do not review the behaviour of concern, but rather, discuss the expected behaviour, new rule, consequences and why it is important. Leave lots of time for asking questions, for role-playing and for obtaining input from your child when appropriate.

If you are feeling hesitant about imposing expectations on your child, remember that you are the parent and you are entitled to make the rules in your home. Plus you are doing this so that life will be easier and more fun for all of you.

Explain the method fully. If you do this, the result will be that you will only have to do it once and you will increase your child's co-operation. If not, it could be pandemonium!

Explain the goal of this approach. Tell him the goal is to teach self-control so that he can do the things that he knows he needs to do. Tell him you know that he doesn't like to be reminded of what to do all the time and you don't like having to remind him. However, you have done it in the past because you didn't know what else to do and it was important to get the job done. Now you are all going to be learning a new way of doing things that will help him be more independent and get you *off his case*. (This part is usually very well received!)

Explain your responsibility to him as his parent. You want to do a good job as a parent and make sure that your child grows up to be the best person he can be. Sometimes people understand that rules are important, but they don't follow the rules because they lack self-control. Your job as a parent is to help him develop self-control so that he can follow the rules at school and in the world and grow up to be an independent and competent adult.

Discuss why rules are important in society. You might explain that, in our society, we have rules so life will run smoothly, so everyone's rights are respected and so people will be safe and able to lead healthy and comfortable lives. Discuss the relationship between our choices to follow the rules and the freedom we have. If we choose to follow rules, we usually have a lot of freedom. If we choose not to follow the rules, we often lose our freedom.

Choose a couple of examples that are meaningful to your child. For instance, people who choose not to pay for what they take out of stores and are caught, usually lose the freedom to go into that store. They might even go to jail. If we choose to pay for what we want, we have the freedom to go back in the store. Notice that we are describing the behaviour we want to see, not the undesirable choices. We do not say, "People who steal."

Driving is another example. When we choose to follow the driving rules, such as stopping at stop lights or driving the speed limit, the consequence is that we can continue to drive without having to pay fines. If we choose not to follow the driving rules and we are caught, the consequence is that we will have to pay fines and we might even lose the freedom to drive for a while.

Kids don't usually think of the positive consequence of choosing to pay for items that we take out of stores or driving according to the rules and neither do a lot of adults. *Riding the Wave* makes the positive consequences of choices much more obvious.

Review the rule and consequences. Now it is time to review the first rule you have chosen and why it is important. You will do this for every new rule. Be open to some negotiation on details of the rule such as deadlines and what else you can do to assist the situation. This might be making charts or arranging for alarm clocks. Whatever you do, reminders from you to start or complete a task are no longer an option.

Go over both positive and negative consequences of the choices. Be open to role-playing so that you can be sure that everything, including the *Back-up Plan*, is perfectly understood. Act it all out, in a non-emotional way, taking turns in different roles. Make sure your child understands your words and is capable of doing the task you are requiring of him. If not, teach him how or adjust your expectations.

Once you have all learned how to do *Riding the Wave* on the first rule, other rules can easily be added. You must be sure to complete the *Behaviour Management Worksheet* for each rule and then explain the rule and consequences to your child, before implementing anything new.

STEP TEN – Pulling it all together: just do it !

Time estimate: This is ongoing and will vary considerably according to your rule and consequences. Generally, reciting your script when you notice your child's positive choice will take five to ten seconds. For a negative consequence, it might take fifteen to thirty minutes to supervise the activities that were not completed.

Directions: Catch your child making choices. Describe what you see your child doing in terms of the choice he has made about whether or not to follow the rule and then indicate the consequence. Be sure to use the script you wrote. There is no need to be creative and there should be no lecturing, no reminding, and no putting it off. Just do it, on time, in a kind, calm, firm, compassionate, and detached manner.

The greatest joy most parents report is that they no longer feel like the bad guy or the Wicked Witch of the West. They are no longer the remote control car driver, chasing their children all the time. They also feel more positive, more relaxed. They can see clearly that their child has made a choice and they are simply in charge of ensuring that the consequences are applied. It is very freeing.

The children appreciate knowing what is going on. The rules are stated ahead of time and the expectations and consequences are clearly understood. They are given an opportunity to experience the results of their choices and they learn quickly.

Once you have completed Steps One to Ten and are confident with using this technique, you can choose to address any behaviour. Complete a new *Behaviour Management Worksheet* and start right away.

Remember that no family should have more than five rules at any one time. It is often too tiring and difficult for the adults to be consistent in noticing all of the choices that are being made. It is also not really necessary to address more than two or three behaviours. Many families see positive results with the very first behaviour they target.

> This technique takes a lot of prior thought in order to make sure that all the bases are covered. However, if it is used properly, it really works!!!

CHAPTER SIX

AVOIDING THE FOUR COMMON PITFALLS

In this section, we review four mistakes that are easy to make. If you know about them ahead of time, you can avoid these common pitfalls.

Common Pitfall #1 - Focusing on the Negative

When generating your rule, you will state what you are expecting and how it applies to the whole family. Part of the power of *Riding the Wave*, is that we are consistently prescribing the positive or what we expect. However, it can be easy to slip into labeling the negative behaviour.

It is important that you do <u>not</u> say, "*I notice you chose to be rude.*" Always use the expected behaviour in your statement. <u>Do</u> say, *"I notice that you chose NOT to be respectful. As a result..."*

Also remember the 3:1 ratio. Notice when your child chooses to follow the rule three times more often than when she chooses <u>not</u> to follow the rule.

Common Pitfall #2 - Making Exceptions

Sometimes we are tempted to make exceptions when the child's behaviour is close to our expectations. This occurs when the job is **almost** done properly -when they have finished most of their homework or have gotten all their clothes on except their socks or have picked up most of their toys. Although we think it might be nice or encouraging to the child to tell them that they have chosen to follow the rule and allow them the positive consequence, the truth is they have actually chosen **not** to follow the rule according to the standard that was set.

If you choose to make an exception in this case, you will find that the next time, your child does less, not more. Making exceptions also puts you back with the remote car controls in hand, attempting to steer and control a disempowered child. If you choose to stay true to the rules and standards, however, your child will most likely rise to the occasion the next time.

You can soften your language somewhat, as in the example below, but still maintain the standard that has been set. This is a slight adaptation to the technique, but it will help you to acknowledge the child's effort while, at the same time, being consistent.

EXAMPLE – SOFTENING THE SCRIPT

The rule is: We tidy up after ourselves.

Positive (+) *If you choose to tidy up after yourself, the consequence is that you have had the freedom to do it independently.*

Negative (-) *If you choose <u>not</u> to tidy up after yourself, the consequence is that you will lose the freedom to do it on your own. Let's go.*

We are sometimes tempted to make exceptions when the child has succeeded picking up almost all of their belongings throughout the house, but may have missed one tiny part (like a toothbrush on the sink). In this case, the task is <u>almost</u> done properly. However, it can seem cruel and inaccurate to use the planned script, *"I notice you chose not to tidy up."* This sometimes happens in the beginning of learning the skill. So you may want to soften your language somewhat and respond with, *"I notice that you chose <u>not</u> to tidy up after yourself completely. The consequence is that you will still need supervision to finish tidying up properly. The good news is that it'll only take a few minutes of supervision before it's done. I'm sure that next time you'll be completely successful and able to do it independently."*

You are not making an exception here, you are softening the script – but this should only be done very occasionally. It is better for you and your child to have set a firm and clear standard that can be met each time.

Common Pitfall #3 - Focusing on the Consequence

Sometimes people do not make the connection between cause and effect. They might say wrongly, *"I notice you chose to be supervised for your chores."*

People do <u>not</u> choose consequences; they make choices that have a particular result or consequence.

Always use the words "chose" and "consequence". Making this connection is what builds self-control, internal monitoring, motivation, responsibility and self-esteem.

Common Pitfall #4 – Overly Helpful Siblings or Classmates

Often siblings or classmates catch on very quickly to the language of rules and consequences. However, they usually notice the choices that others make when they have chosen <u>not</u> to follow the rule and make a comment about it. This violates the 3:1 Positive/Negative guideline used in **Riding the Wave**. Therefore, we encourage parents and teachers to post the following rule: *"Friends are Strength Detectors![6] They notice the good choices others are making."*

In this case, children are told that the adults are in charge of using the language of choice and consequence as outlined in **Riding the Wave**. However, others can serve an important role as a Strength Detector, learning to notice when positive behaviours have been made. For instance, "I really like the way that you tidied up your toys!" If a sibling or classmate notices when someone has <u>not</u> followed the rule and they make a comment to that effect, the child being observed is given permission to ignore the comment.

---

[6] Thanks to Dr. Ilze Matiss for suggesting the term "Strength Detectors."

Some Gentle Reminders

❖ When learning how to use the ***Riding the Wave*** method, begin to work on <u>only one</u> behaviour at a time. You will definitely <u>not</u> work on the one that bothers you the most. Remember the ripple effect? Starting with only <u>one</u> behaviour will result in changes in other areas. After you have learned how to use this method, you can choose whatever behaviour you wish.

❖ It is important to take the time to properly prepare before introducing this to your family. This is your homework. You may be eager to begin, but proper preparation is essential to the success of this approach.

❖ Once you have selected a behaviour to focus on, be sure to completely fill out a *Behaviour Management Worksheet* on that particular behaviour. Any of the examples in this book will show you how to complete it effectively.

❖ Make good use of checklists and charts to support your routines.

❖ Be sure to adapt the suggestions to what fits for you.

❖ Don't promise if you can't deliver the consequences.

❖ Use the "language of choice" and verbally notice the cause-effect relationships. (e.g., "Debbie, I notice that you have chosen to take care of your belongings. The consequence is that you will have access to your belongings tomorrow.")

❖ Making the effort to notice the positives will have a powerful effect on self-esteem. The cause-effect connection teaches self-control. The use of this method will help you to feel that you are doing something within your power to help the situation.

CHAPTER SEVEN

WHERE DO WE GO FROM HERE?

Within a few months of implementing ***Riding the Wave***, you will begin to notice that your child is learning self-control. Even using one or two rules and consistently noticing your child's choices will strengthen the cause-effect connection and build self-control and self-esteem. It has been my professional experience that two-thirds of the original behaviours of concern simply disappear without direct targeting.

Parents learn that as their child's behaviour and consistency in following the established rules improves, they still need to notice when their child makes choices with positive consequences. Some parents get such great results with the ***Riding the Wave*** approach that they quickly forget about noticing the positives. Pretty soon the child's behaviour of concern is back to where it was before they started the program. If this happens to you, all you have to do is look up the original rule and begin again; making sure that you consistently find ways to notice the positive three times more often than the negative.

I have also watched as parents successfully learn how to *catch the child being good*, while highlighting the *cause-effect* connection. Before implementing ***Riding the Wave,*** the parent might have said, "Good job!" or "I really like the way you are taking care of your toys!" Now they make the connection between the child's choice and the positive consequences and say, "When you choose to take care of your toys, the result is that they last longer" or "When you choose to always tell the truth, the result is that I believe what you say." Parents are soon able to use the cause-effect connection more informally as they weave in comments like these spontaneously without requiring a separate rule and a prescribed script. These positive comments about their child's choices are also going a long way towards building a positive parent/child relationship.

A positive parent/child relationship is an essential foundation to the successful application of the *Riding the Wave* approach and the future success of your child. During my first session working with new clients I often say, "Because you have chosen to take the time to learn *Riding the Wave*, the consequence is that life is going to get a lot easier for you." It is usually the case.

I trust that it will be for you too!

APPENDIX A

BLANK FORMS & WORKSHEETS

Behaviours of Concern

Behaviours of Concern	Situation (when and where and what time of day the behaviour occurs)

Things I like about My Child and Ways I am a Good Parent

Things I like about my child

Ways I am a good parent

Responding to My Child's Behaviour

Positive Behaviours		Negative Behaviours	
What's working now?		*What's not working yet?*	
What did my child do?	*How did I respond?*	*What did my child do?*	*How did I respond?*

Is this a typical sample of my interaction with my child? _____

Behaviour Management Worksheet

Selected behaviour of concern
Expected behaviour
Rule Stated in the positive, applied to the whole family
Consequences   **Positive (+)** _____   **Negative (-)** _____   **Script (+)** _____   _____   _____   **Script (-)** _____   _____   _____
What else can I do to help the situation?   _____   _____   **Back-up Plan**   _____   _____

THIS FORM MAY BE REPRODUCED FOR PERSONAL USE

EXAMPLES OF COMPLETED BEHAVIOUR MANAGEMENT WORKSHEETS

Appendix B contains examples of completed *Behaviour Management Worksheets* that provide just one way of dealing with a behaviour of concern. If you are working on a particular issue, you will need to find what works best in your own family situation.

Example #1 - Age Range: Preschool

Selected behaviour of concern *Hitting siblings*
Expected behaviour *4-year old Ryan plays nicely with his little sister Sally.*
Rule *We use gentle touch.*
Consequences **Positive (+)** *You have freedom to continue playing with her.* **Negative (-)** *You lose the freedom to play with Sally for five minutes.* **Script** **(+)** *Ryan, I notice that you chose to use gentle touch with Sally. The consequence is that you have freedom to continue playing with her.* **(-)** *Ryan, I notice that you chose <u>not</u> to use gentle touch with Sally. The consequence is that you have lost the freedom to play with Sally for five minutes. I'll let you know when five minutes is up and you can come back and play again.*
What else can I do to help the situation? *Teach the meaning of the word "consequence" when explaining the new system. Practice <u>how</u> to touch gently and how to ask for what he needs instead of grabbing.*
Back-up Plan **Rule** *We co-operate with the negative consequences (i.e., time out).* **(+)** *The consequence is over quickly and you can continue to play.* **(-)** *The consequence is not over quickly. The buzzer is reset for another five minutes and you lose the freedom to continue to play. No more TV or videogames for the rest of the day.*

Example #2 - Age Range: School Age

Selected behaviour of concern *Not getting ready for school on time 6-year old Charlotte plays with her toys when she should be getting ready for school.*

Expected behaviour *Charlotte gets ready for school without being reminded.*

Rule *We get ready on time. (Charlotte will be ready for school by 7:30 am.)*

Consequences

Positive (+) *You have the freedom to get ready on your own.*

Negative (-) *You lose the freedom to get ready on your own. My hands will have to help you.*

Script

(+) *Charlotte, I notice that you chose to get ready for school on time. The consequence is that you have had the freedom to do it on your own.*

(-) *Charlotte, I notice that you chose not to get ready for school on time. The consequence is that you have lost the freedom to do it on your own. My hands will have to help you. Let's go.*

What else can I do to help the situation? *Have the child choose clothes the night before, making sure you leave enough time to get her ready if necessary. Make up a chart of what is involved in "Getting Ready for the Day" and post this in the washroom and on the fridge. (Kids often like to color or decorate their own charts.)*

Back-up Plan

Rule *We co-operate with the negative consequence.*

(+) *If she chooses to co-operate in getting ready while you are supervising her getting ready, the consequence is that she will have the freedom to play freely for the rest of the morning (i.e., watch TV, play with all her toys).*

(-) *If she chooses not to co-operate, she will lose the freedom to play video games or watch TV for the rest of the morning.*

Example #3 - Age Range: Adolescent

Selected behaviour of concern *15-year old Peter doesn't finish his homework.*

Expected behaviour *Peter starts and completes his homework on time.*

Rule *We finish our work on time. For Peter, this means homework is finished by 8 pm. Explain that we all have "work" and for Peter, it is starting and completing his homework by 8 pm.*

Consequences

Positive (+) *You have the freedom to do your homework in your own way. (That is, with the TV or computer on, in the kitchen or living room, with assistance from parents, etc.)*

Negative (-) *You lose the freedom to do your homework in your own way. Now, we'll do it my way (after 8 pm I decide where and how you do your homework and I will watch you do it.).*

Script

(+) *Peter, I notice that you have chosen to finish your homework on time. As a result, you have had the freedom to do it in your own way.*

(-) *Peter, I notice that you have chosen <u>not</u> to finish your homework on time. As a result, you have lost the freedom to do it in your own way.*

What else can I do to help the situation? *Make up a daily schedule chart that includes homework time and the steps involved. Steps on a chart might be: 1. Plan homework. 2. Do homework. 3. Check homework. 4. Show parent completed homework. 5. Play. (You might also want to make sure that he is capable of doing the work. If writing or spelling is difficult for him, arrange to have him dictate his answers to you or use a computer with a spell-checker).*

Back-up Plan *If he chooses to co-operate with the consequence of doing his homework your way, the consequence is that he will be finished sooner. If he chooses <u>not</u> to co-operate with you, the consequence is that it will take him longer to finish his homework and he will lose the freedom to use his free time as he wishes for the rest of the evening. You will need to decide and then make it very clear what is allowed and what isn't.*

Example #4: Age Range: Adolescent

Selected behaviour of concern *Not coming home on time: 16-year old Leila stays out past her curfew.*

Expected behaviour *Leila comes home by her curfew – 10 pm on weeknights and midnight on weekends.*

Rule *We come home on time.*

Consequences

Positive (+) *You have the freedom to go out tomorrow night.*

Negative (-) *You lose the freedom to go out tomorrow. You can try again the next day.*

Script

(+) Leila, I notice that you chose to come home on time. The consequence is that you have the freedom to go out tomorrow night.

(-) Leila, I notice that you choose <u>not</u> to come home on time. The consequence is that you have lost the freedom to go out tomorrow.

What else can I do to help the situation? *Negotiate a reasonable curfew - probably different for weekdays and weekends, arrangements for letting you know where she is and how much time she will have to allow in order to ensure that she makes it home by curfew. What if she is five minutes late or she misses her bus? You may want to consider some of the following options. If she comes in very close to curfew time, but still late, you might want to figure out how you will be kind and encouraging while remaining consistent with the decided consequences. Or maybe she is allowed to go out on only one weekend night until she shows that she is going to respect the family guidelines. If you talk about this ahead of time, it will prevent a lot of worry and late night negotiating over the phone.*

Back-up Plan *If she chooses to respect the guidelines, the rules stay the same. If she chooses <u>not</u> to respect the guidelines, the rules tighten up. You will need to decide and then specify how the rules will change. Curfew might be earlier and there might be no going out during the week.*

RIDING THE WAVE

Appendix B

Example #5 - Age Range: Adolescent or Adult

Selected behaviour of concern *Being verbally abusive - Pascal yells and screams and calls me names when I say something he disagrees with.*

Expected behaviour *Pascal expresses his feelings and opinion in a normal tone of voice.*

Rule *We treat each other with respect.*

Consequences

Positive (+) *You have the freedom to be with me.*

Negative (-) *You lose the freedom to be with me for 5 minutes.*

Script

(+) *Pascal, I notice that you are choosing to treat me with respect. The consequence is that you have the freedom to be with me.*

(-) *Pascal, I notice that you chose <u>not</u> to treat me with respect. The consequence is that you have lost the freedom to be with me for 5 minutes. Bye-bye.*

What else can I do to help the situation? *Make sure that Pascal knows how to express his feelings in an appropriate way. "I-messages"[7] are a safe and effective way to say how you are feeling without being disrespectful. They follow the formula "I feel (state your emotion) when you (state the behaviour)." An example would be "I feel angry when you tell me that I can't have the car." Once someone has given an I-message, be sure that the other person knows how to really listen to the feelings that have been expressed. For instance, the listener would say "You feel really mad when I won't let you do something you really want to do." This is called "active listening" and needs to be used when someone gives an "I-message."*

---

[7] See Faber A. (1999) *How to Talk so Kids will Listen & Listen so Kids Will Talk* (in the Selected Reading List at the end of this book)

81

Example #6 - Age Range: Spouse or Partner

Selected behaviour of concern *Teeya is late when leaving for Church.*

Expected behaviour *Teeya is ready to leave on time.*

Rule *We are in the car on time (10:15 am).*

Consequences

Positive (+) *We can go together in Nico's car.*

Negative (-) *We cannot go together. You'll have to take your own car and your carbon footprint will increase considerably. Bye!*

Script

(+) Teeya, I notice that you chose to be in the car on time. As a result, we can drive together.

(-) Teeya, I notice that you chose <u>not</u> to be in the car on time. As a result, we can't go together. You'll have to take your own car. Bye!

What else can I do to help the situation?

Be sure that the leaving time is firmly established well in advance and agreed upon by both parties.

APPENDIX C

CHART OF BEHAVIOURS OF CONCERN, RULES & CONSEQUENCES

The information on this chart is intended as a reference list only so that you don't have to reinvent the wheel in coming up with positive and negative consequences for your child's choices. These behaviours are not listed in any particular order. You will need to find a behaviour that is close to the one you are working on and then adapt the suggested rules and consequences to your own family, routine, and preferences while filling out the *Behaviour Management Worksheet* (Step Seven).

	Behaviour of Concern	**Expected Behaviour/Rule**		**Consequences**
1	Not getting up when alarm goes off	We get up when our alarm rings.	(+)	Get up on our own
			(-)	Require assistance (e.g. wet washcloth on face)
2	Not getting dressed in the morning	We get dressed by 7:30 am.	(+)	Choose own clothes and get self dressed
			(-)	I choose your clothes and get you dressed
3	Not doing chores	We do our chores.	(+)	Freedom to act independently
			(-)	Lose freedom to act independently (e.g. require supervision until done)
4	Yells, swears, or hits others	We treat each other with respect.	(+)	Freedom to be with each other
			(-)	Lose freedom to be with each other for 5 minutes.
5	Not getting ready on time	We get ready by 8:15 am.	(+)	Freedom to get ready on your own
			(-)	Lose freedom to get ready on your own (e.g. "I will supervise you")

	Behaviour of Concern	**Expected Behaviour/Rule**		**Consequences**
6	Not coming home on time	We come home on time.	(+)	Freedom to go out the next day
			(-)	Lose the freedom to go out the next day
7	Not bringing homework home	We bring homework home.	(+)	Get to do assigned work which helps us with lessons
			(-)	Get to do work "invented" by parents
8	Not starting homework on own	We start homework at 7 pm.	(+)	You may do it wherever you wish
			(-)	You lose the freedom to choose the location and I will decide where you do it
9	Not finishing homework	We finish homework by 9 pm.	(+)	Get to do it independently
			(-)	Lose freedom to do it independently – I will supervise you
10	Doing homework in a messy way	We do our work well.	(+)	It's done and we're free to play
			(-)	It will need to be redone until it's neat

	Behaviour of Concern	Expected Behaviour/Rule		Consequences
11	Leaves kitchen a mess	We clean up after ourselves.	(+)	We clean up independently
			(-)	We lose the freedom to clean up independently (e.g. require supervision while doing so)
12	Not doing a good job on face, teeth, etc.	We groom ourselves properly.	(+)	Do it on your own
			(-)	Lose the freedom to do it on your own
13	Not eating food at mealtime	We eat what's put on our plates.	(+)	Opportunity to eat on your own
			(-)	Lose freedom to eat on your own (e.g. "I will feed you")
14	Throws toys, rips books	We take care of our belongings.	(+)	Continued access to your belongings
			(-)	Lose access to your belongings for a day

	Behaviour of Concern	**Expected Behaviour/Rule**		**Consequences**
15	Playing instead of eating breakfast	Breakfast is finished by 8 am.	(+)	Freedom to eat on your own
			(-)	Lose freedom to eat on your own (e.g. "1 will feed you")
16	Noisy in the house	We play quietly inside.	(+)	Freedom to play inside if you wish
			(-)	Lose freedom to play inside (e.g. must go outside for 5 min.)
17	Not wearing seatbelts	We wear seatbelts in the car.	(+)	We can drive
			(-)	We don't drive until your seatbelt is done up
18	Asking for things while shopping	We ask for a treat only when we are done shopping.	(+)	You may choose a treat when we're done
			(-)	You lose the chance for a treat when we are done
19	Running away in malls	We stay with our parent in malls.	(+)	Walk by yourself
			(-)	Lose freedom to walk by yourself self (e.g." hold my hand for 5 minutes")

	Behaviour of Concern	Expected Behaviour/Rule		Consequences
20	Lying/not telling the truth	We tell the truth.	(+)	I believe what you tell me
			(-)	I can't believe what you say unless you can prove it
21	Stealing/taking things	We pay for what we take.	(+)	Freedom to go into stores
			(-)	Lose freedom to go into stores
22	Not returning borrowed items	We return what we borrow.	(+)	Freedom to continue borrowing
			(-)	Lose freedom to borrow for a day
23	Not washing hair properly	We groom ourselves well.	(+)	Freedom to do it on your own
			(-)	Lose freedom to do it yourself
24	Not staying in bed	We stay in bed at night.	(+)	Go to bed at the same time
			(-)	Go to bed 15 minutes earlier tomorrow night

	Behaviour of Concern	Expected Behaviour/Rule		Consequences
25	Not getting ready for bed	We get ready for bed by 8 pm.	(+)	Can get ready on your own
			(-)	Lose freedom to do it for yourself (e.g. "I will do it for you")
26	Asks for spending money	We get money each week when we are paid our allowance.	(+)	We get our whole allowance
			(-)	We don't get our whole allowance (as you lose 5 cents every time you ask for money)
27	Leaves towels on floor	We leave the bathroom tidy.	(+)	We clean up independently
			(-)	We lose the freedom to clean up independently (e.g. require supervision while doing so)
28	Not taking medication	We look after ourselves.	(+)	We function independently
			(-)	We require parental supervision
29	Not keeping promises	We do the things we promise.	(+)	We have the freedom to do it our own way
			(-)	We lose the freedom to do it our own way (e.g. require supervision)

RESOURCES

Children and Adults with Attention Deficit/Hyperactivity Disorder (CHADD) – A charitable organization that aims to help support, educate, and ultimately better the lives of individuals with ADHD, and those who care for them.

CHADD Canada - http://www.chaddcanada.org/

Chapters

CHADD Calgary

Coordinator: Roberta Funk

Contact: chaddcalgary@yahoo.com

Website: http://members.shaw.ca/chaddcalgary/

CHADD Edmonton Satellite Chapter

Contact: chaddedmontonsatellite@yahoo.ca

Facilitator: Rachel Rogers

CHADD Vancouver

Coordinator: Carol Walley

Contact: chaddvan@vcn.bc.ca

Website: http://www.vcn.bc.ca/chaddvan/

CHADD North Van Satellite Chapter

Contact: fbjones@shaw.ca

http://www.chadd.org/

CHADD United States

National Resource Center on AD/HD - call 800-233-4050

To find your local chapter:

http://www.chadd.org/AM/Template.cfm?Section=Find_Local_CHADD_Chapters&
Template=/CustomPages/ChapterLocator/findchap.cfm

Learning Disability Association (LDAC)

LDAC Canada

http://www.ldac-acta.ca/

Call toll-free 1-877-238-5332

Email: info@ldac-acta.ca

613-238-5721

LDA Alberta

P.O. Box 29011, Lendrum P.O., Edmonton, AB T6H 5Z6

Tel: (780) 448-0360 *Toll free in Alberta only: 1-877-238-5322*

General Inquiries: info@ldaa.ca

Website: www.ldaa.ca

Local chapters: http://www.ldaa.ca/aboutus/networks.aspx

LDA British Columbia

Suite #513, 7360 137th Street, Surrey, BC V3W 1A3

Tel: (604) 591-5156

Toll free in BC only: 1-877-238-5322

General Inquiries: vicki.n@ldabc.ca

Website: www.ldabc.ca

Local chapters: http://www.ldabc.ca/our-organization/find-a-chapter/

LDA Manitoba

617 Erin Street, Winnipeg, MN R3G 2W1
Tel: (204) 774-1821
Toll free in Manitoba only: 1-877-238-5322
Fax: (204) 788-4090

General Inquiries: ldamb@mts.net
Website: http://www.ldamanitoba.org/
Local chapters: http://www.ldamanitoba.org/contact.htm

LDA New Brunswick

203-403 Regent Street, Fredericton, NB E3B 3X6
Tel: (506) 459-7852
Toll free in NB only: 1-877-544-7852
Fax:(506) 455-9300
General Inquiries:ldanb_taanb@nb.aibn.com
Website:http://www.nald.ca/ldanb/english/home.htm

LDA Newfoundland and Labrador

66 Kenmount Road, Suite 204, St. John's, NL A1B 3V7
Tel: (709) 753-1445
Toll free in NF only: 1-877-238-5322
Fax: (709) 753-4747
General Inquiries:ldanl@nl.rogers.com
Website: http://www.nald.ca/ldanl/main.asp

LDA Nova Scotia

46 Portland Street, Suite 601, Dartmouth, NS B2Y 1H4
Tel: (902) 423-2850
Toll free in NS only:1-877-238-5322
Fax:(902) 423-2834
General Inquiries:info@ldans.ca
Website: http://www.ldans.ca/

LDA Ontario

365 Bloor Street East, Suite 1004, Box 39,Toronto, ON M4W 3L4

Tel: (416) 929-4311

Toll free in Ontario only:1-877-238-5322

Fax: (416) 929-3905

General Inquiries:dianew@ldao.ca

Website:www.ldao.ca

Local chapters: http://www.ldao.ca/aboutLDAO/chapters.php

LDA Prince Edward Island

40 Enman Crescent, Room 149, Charlottetown PE C1E 1E6

Tel: (902) 894-5032

Toll free in PEI only: 1-877-238-5322

General Inquiries: ldapei@eastlink.ca

Website: http://www.ldapei.ca/

LDA Quebec

284 Notre Dame Ouest, Suite 300, Montréal, QC H2Y 1T7

Tel: (514) 847-1324

Toll free in Quebec only: 1-877-238-5322

Fax: (514) 281-5187

General Inquiries: info@aqeta.qc.ca

Website: http://www.aqeta.qc.ca/fr

Local chapters: http://www.aqeta.qc.ca/fr/contactez_nous/sections

LDA Saskatchewan

3 – 701 Second Ave N, Saskatoon SK S7K 2C9

Tel: (306) 652-4114

Toll free in SK only: 1-877-238-5322

Fax: (306) 652-3220

General Inquiries: reception@ldas.org

Website: www.ldas.org
Local chapters: http://www.ldas.org/contactus.aspx

LDA Yukon

107 Main Street, Whitehorse YT, Y1A 2A7, Canada
Tel: 867-668-5167
Toll free in Yukon only: 1-877-238-5322
Fax: 867-668-6504
General Inquiries: ldayoffice@northwestel.net
Website: http://www.nald.ca/litweb/province/yt/lday/index.htm

Learning Disability Association of America

http://www.ldanatl.org/

Phone (412) 341-1515 Fax (412) 344-0224

Locate state chapters: http://www.ldanatl.org/state_chapters/index.asp

SELECTED READING LIST

Alexander-Roberts, C. (1995). *ADHD and Teens: A Parent's Guide to Making it Through the Tough Years*. Dallas, TX: Taylor Publishing.

> A practical book with a very realistic approach to parenting and the issues of adolescence. Good for a parent of any teen.

Blakemore, B., Shindler, S. and Conte, R. (1993). A Problem-Solving Training Program for Parents of Children with Attention Deficit Hyperactivity Disorder. *Canadian Journal of School Psychology*, 2 (1),66-85.

> A journal article describing the original 12-week program which formed the basis for **Riding the Wave,** the behaviour management technique described in this book.

Faber, Adele, Mazlish, Elaine (1999). *How to Talk so Kids Will Listen and Listen So Kids Will Talk*. New York, N.Y. Rawson, Wade Publishers.

Hallowell, E.M.& Ratey, J.M. (2010). *Answers to Distraction*. New York: Anchor.

> Full of practical suggestions.

Hartmann, T. (1997). *Attention Deficit Disorder: A Different Perception*. Nevada City, CA: Underwood Books.

> Discusses the adaptability of individuals with A.D.D. and compares them to "hunters" who are living in a "farmer" environment.

Johnson, C. (1992). *Captain Chaos Lives Here! A Survival Guide for Parents Raising Very Active Children*. Calgary, AB: Chaos Consultation and Training.

> A cute little book that has lots of practical suggestions for the young, very active child with AD/HD who experiences organizational challenges!

Kelly, K. and Ramundo. P. (2006). *You Mean I'm Not Lazy, Stupid or Crazy?!:The Classic Self-Help Book for Adults with Attention Deficit Disorder*. New York: Scribner.

> An up-beat book about the author's process of self-discovery of A.D.D., includes lots of practical tips for organizational challenges.

Kurcinka, M. S. (1998) *Raising Your Spirited Child*, New York, Harper-Collins.

> An essential guideline for identifying how intense, perceptive, sensitive, persistent or energetic your child is and how to work best with her.

Moss, R. A. (1995). *Why Johnny Can't Concentrate: Coping With Attention Deficit Problems*. New York: Bantam Books.

> An easy-to-read book that covers A.D.D. across the lifespan with or without hyperactivity.

Nadeau, K. (2006). *Survival Guide for College Students with A.D.D. or L.D.* Washington, DC: Magination Press.

> An easy-to-read book, full of practical tips for managing in postsecondary settings.

Nadeau, K., Dixon, E. and Biggs, S. (2000). *School Strategies for ADD Teens*. Altamonte Springs, FL:Advantage Books.

> A wonderful resource that reviews many learning strategies useful to high school and post-secondary students.

Scholten, T. (2010). *The A.D.D. Guidebook: A Self-Directed Guide to Understanding A.D.D. in Adults and Children. 3rd Edition*. Calgary, AB: Scholten Psychological Services Press.

> Written in a positive, user-friendly style, this book outlines a wholistic approach to investigating "Attention Deluxe Dimension".

Scholten, T. (2002). *Turning the Tides: Teaching the Student with A.D.D.* Calgary, AB: Scholten Psychological Services Press.

> Part One reviews a number of factors that should be considered by teachers when they are concerned about attention difficulties in their students. Part Two describes the behaviour management approach **Riding the Wave**, as adapted to educational settings.

Scholten, T. (2002). *Welcome to the Channel-surfers' Club,* Calgary, AB: Scholten Psychological Services Press.

> Written for children who have just been diagnosed with ADD or AD/HD explaining how it can be an advantage to have a channel-surfing brain.

Scholten, T. and Dunning, D. 2nd Edition (2008). *Ready-Set-Go: A Three-Step Problem-Solving Process for Improved Learning Performance.* Red Deer, AB: Unlimited Learning.

> Illustrates the use of a cost-effective positive problem-solving model as a method for clarifying and addressing concerns with students.

Weiss, L. (2005). *Attention Deficit Disorder in Adults*. Dallas, Texas: Taylor Trade Publishing Co.

> Contains a checklist of attention symptoms and information to help the adult reader deal with A.D.D. in a positive manner.

ABOUT THE AUTHOR

Dr. Teeya Scholten is a Registered Psychologist who has been working in the field of education and mental health for over 25 years. She runs a successful private practice in Calgary, Alberta, Canada where she specializes in the areas of learning, attention and depression in adults, adolescents and children. She offers a variety of services, including consultation, assessment and individual counselling, behaviour management programs for teachers and parents of children with A.D.D., and in-service training in the form of workshops and consultations to other professionals. She has published in the areas of consultation, assessment and program planning for individuals with learning and attentional challenges. Dr. Teeya is committed to the empowerment of clients and professionals and believes in the importance of Body, Mind and Spirit integration in order to maximize one's potential. She has developed Empowerment Plus® which is a cost-effective model of psychological service delivery. Training is available to qualified practitioners upon request. Contact her at www.GoodNewsAboutADD.com for more information.

THE *RIDING THE WAVE* FEEDBACK FORM

1.   How did you find out about *Riding the Wave*?

2.   What did you like best about it?

3.   What didn't you like about it?

4.   What role do you have in relation to A.D.D.?   Are you a:
(Check all the roles that apply to you and put a star * beside your primary concern, at this time.)

    ☐ person with ADD
    ☐ parent of a child with ADD
    ☐ partner of a person with ADD
    ☐ professional working with clients with A.D.D.
     (Please specify type of professional: physician __ , psychologist ___ ,
     social worker ___other _____)
    ☐ someone who knows a family with A.D.D. and wants to learn more
    ☐ someone who has a friend with A.D.D. and wants to learn more
    ☐ other (Please specify_____)

5.   Do you have any additional comments or suggestions?

THANKS FOR TAKING THE TIME TO PROVIDE FEEDBACK!

Dr. Teeya Scholten, R. Psych.
Box# 923, 105 – 150 Crowfoot Cr. NW, Calgary AB T3G 3T2
Phone: (403) 239-8597
e-mail: teeya@shaw.ca
www.GoodNewsAboutADD.com

Empowerment Plus® Product Order Form

Description	Qty.	Price	Subtotal	Discount*
Books				
Attention Deluxe Dimension**	____	$15.00	_____	_____
The A.D.D. Guidebook	____	$35.00	_____	_____
Riding the Wave	____	$20.00	_____	_____
Turning the Tides	____	$30.00	_____	_____
Welcome to the Channel-surfers' Club!**	____	$15.00	_____	_____
Ready-Set-Go	____	$20.00	_____	_____
Overcoming Depression	____	$40.00	_____	_____
Video				
Empowerment Plus® 15 min. DVD	____	$10.00	_____	
Empowerment Plus® Training Materials				
Manual	____	$45.00	_____	
Forms Book (with CD)	____	$25.00	_____	
NRSI Fan of 8-Coloured Overlays	____	$15.00	_____	
Files with Forms	____	$10.00	_____	
Resource Manual	____	$125.00	_____	

Order Sub-Total _____

Shipping and Handling - Add 20% of Order Sub-Total, Minimum $5.00 _____

FINAL TOTAL _____

To purchase materials, Mail or Fax completed Product Order Form with payment to address or Fax # listed below. Allow three weeks for delivery. All prices are quoted in Canadian funds, subject to change without notice.

(Online Shopping Cart coming soon!)

Name: _____

Address:_____

_____

_____

Phone: _____ Email: _____

Method of Payment

☐ Cheque - Payable to Dr. Teeya Scholten   ☐ Money Order   ☐ Purchase Order #_____

Credit Card #: _____ Exp. date_____   ☐ Visa

Signature: _____   ☐ MasterCard

*   35% discount on books and video to those Certified at Levels I, I/II or III

**   These books are also available as FREE downloads from the website (see below)

Empowerment Plus® International, Inc.
Suite 923, 105 - 150 Crowfoot Cres. N.W.
Calgary, Alberta, Canada T3G 3T2
www.TheGoodNewsAboutADD.com

Tel 403.829.3441
Fax 403.547.4288
Toll Free 888-DrTeeya (378-3392)
Email: teeya@shaw.ca